AF487043

The MAN GOD CALLED Father

Reprinted with kind permission of

The Blue Army
The World Apostolate of Fatima

Edited by

Helen Miller

Promise of Peace 1917

Paperback ISBN: 979-8-8691-3204-8

CONTENTS

ST. JOSEPH AND THE CHILD JESUS

This booklet is a summary of all the parts describing the life of Saint Joseph which are found in the four-volume Marian revelation, CITY OF GOD. However, while this booklet is a summary of those parts, much is verbatim, such as all quoted conversation. Because CITY OF GOD is an incomparable work designed to honor the Mother of God, the words "Her" and "She" are capitalized throughout this summary.

✳ APPROBATIONS

The first Pope officially to take notice of "Ciudad de Dios" was Pope Innocent XI, who, on July 3, 1686, in response to a series of virulent attacks and machinations of some members of the Sorbonne, known to be Jansenists, issued a breve permitting the publication and reading of the "Ciudad de Dios." Similar decrees were afterward issued by Popes Alexander VIII, Clement IX and Benedict XIII. These decrees were followed by two decrees of the Congregation of Rites, approved by Benedict XIV and Clement XIV, in which the authenticity of "Ciudad de Dios" as extant and written by the Venerable Servant of God, Mary of Jesus, is officially established. The great Pope Benedict XIII, when he was Archbishop of Benevent, used these revelations as material for a series of sermons on the Blessed Virgin. On Sept. 26, 1713, the Bishop of Ceneda, Italy, objecting to the publication of the "City of God," was peremptorily ordered by the Holy Office to withdraw his objections as interfering with the decree of Pope Innocent XI for the Universal Church.

Mary of Agreda, the author, has been declared Venerabilis by the Church, and her writings have been declared free from error. Her body is preserved incorrupt in Agreda.[1] Her work, THE

CITY OF GOD, has appeared in over sixty editions in Spanish, Italian, French, Portuguese, German, Latin, Arabic, Greek, Polish and English.

* * *

On April 29, 1929, Pope Pius XI, granted a private audience to the publisher of THE CITY OF GOD. Referring to the English translation, His Holiness said: "You have done a great work in honor of the Mother of God; she will never permit herself to be outdone in generosity and will know how to reward a thousand-fold . . . We grant the Apostolic Benediction to all readers and promoters of THE CITY OF GOD."

* * *

The Mother of God has deigned to reveal to mankind the entire story of her life on earth with Jesus Christ, as well as what transpired after her death, when she was taken into heaven, body and soul, and crowned by the Most Holy Trinity. This is the only complete history of the Holy Virgin's sojourn on earth, as told by Mary herself, to a Franciscan nun of 17th Century Spain, Venerable Mother Mary of Jesus of Agreda.

* * *

This work also reveals the date and details of the creation of the world, the explanation of the Apocalypse, the details of Lucifer's rebellion and the location of hell. It reveals intimately the hidden life of Jesus, Mary and Joseph, their ages, the death of St. Joseph, the death and burial of the Most Blessed Mary; the death of Herod, Judas, St. Stephen and St. James; the intimate details of the conception, birth, passion and death of Jesus; the number of blows at the scourging; the conversion of St. Paul; the consultations held by the hellish foes against the Blessed Virgin and the Church; the destruction of the temple of Diana by Holy Mary, and much more.

* * *

MODERN MAN NEEDS WHAT *Saint Joseph* HAD

Saint Joseph, at his betrothal to the Blessed Virgin Mary, was thirty-three years old, handsome, pleasing of countenance, modest, grave; chaste in thought and conduct (he made and kept a vow of chastity from his twelfth year). Joseph (as was Mary) was of the race of David and the tribe of Juda.

One day he "assembled with other specially chosen men in the temple where one of them was to be chosen as the Blessed Virgin's spouse. He alone thought himself unworthy, and moreover, not forgetting his vow of chastity, abandoned all to God's will. Although all the men held a rod in their hands, Joseph's alone blossomed. A dove rested on his head, and God interiorly spoke to him: "Joseph, my servant, Mary shall be thy Spouse; accept Her with attentive reverence, for She is acceptable in My eyes, just and most pure in soul and body, and thou shalt do all that She shall say to thee..."

Entering more beautiful than an angel, Mary was espoused to Joseph by priests. Sorrowfully leaving the temple

wherein She had spent a life consecrated to God since the age of three, but sacrificing Her inclinations, Mary, with Joseph, started for Nazareth.

There followed joyful congratulations by friends. Later, left alone, Joseph speaks; "My Spouse and Lady, I give thanks to the Lord most high God for the favor of having designed me as your husband without my merits, though I judged myself unworthy even of thy company; but His Majesty, who can raise up the lowly whenever He wishes, showed this mercy to me, and I desire and hope, relying on thy discretion and virtue, that thou help me to make a proper return in serving Him with an upright heart. Hold me, therefore, as thy servant, and by the true love which I have for thee, I beg of thee to supply my deficiencies in the fulfillment of the domestic duties and other things, which as a worthy husband, I should know how to perform; tell me Lady, what is thy pleasure, in order that I may fulfill it."

The Blessed Virgin Mary humbly and earnestly spoke of Her desire to keep Her perpetual vow of chastity whereby She had consecrated body and soul to God, Her Spouse and Lord. She asked Joseph likewise to offer this acceptable sacrifice to God and promised him Her faithful services.

Joyfully Joseph answered: "My Mistress, in making known to me thy chaste and welcome sentiments, thou hast penetrated and dilated my heart. I have not opened my thoughts to thee before knowing thy own. I also acknowledge myself under greater obligation to the Lord of Creation than other men; for very early He has called me by His true enlightenment to love Him with an upright heart; and I desire thee to know, Lady, that at the age of twelve years I also made a promise to serve the Most High in perpetual chastity. On this account I now gladly ratify this vow in order not to impede thy own; in the presence of His Majesty I promise to aid thee, as far as in me lies, in serving Him and loving Him according to thy full desires. I will be, with the divine grace, thy most faithful servant and companion, and I pray thee accept my chaste love and hold me as thy brother, without ever entertaining any other kind of love, outside the one which thou owest to God and after God to me."

God confirmed his virtue of chastity and also his pure and holy love due Mary. God gave him complete command over his natural inclinations, so that without trace of sensual desires, he might serve Her.

Poor in earthly possessions, Joseph took up his former trade as carpenter. In their humility both tried to obey each other, but Mary won since in the divine plan the man was the natural head of the house. Joseph tried in every way to find Her desires and to please them. Saint Joseph thanked God continuously for such a companion so far above his merits.

Having learned from God that She was to visit Saint Elizabeth in order to aid her in the birth of her son, Saint John the Baptist, the Blessed Virgin asked the consent of Saint Joseph. Joseph said he knew She always inclined to the will of God and therefore gladly consented to Her going, and that he would accompany her. He prepared a few provisions and borrowed a beast of burden.

It was a rough trip to mountainous Judea, and many times Mary dismounted to let Joseph ride but he would not; sometimes he permitted Her to walk beside him in better terrain. Sometimes silent, sometimes talking with Mary on the mystery of the Incarnation (not knowing yet of Her miraculous conception) he continued the journey. In all things he was most solicitous towards his Spouse. He was naturally of a most noble and courteous disposition, his manner most pleasing and charming, and all this was increased by the great holiness received from God due to his privileged position as spouse and protector of the Mother of God.

The journey lasted four days. Kindness here, rudeness there, often met them on the way and always Mary (even then a Mediatrix) and Joseph sought to help anyone they could. They arrived at the town of Juda (in the province of Juda). Joseph went ahead and saluted Elizabeth's family, thereupon Elizabeth and a few of her household issued forth to greet Mary. Saint Joseph returned home to his work till Mary needed his help in returning home.

After the birth of Saint John the Baptist, and after many other mysterious and wonderful developments accompanying Mary's visit, Saint Joseph was informed by Elizabeth that it was time to take Mary home. Zachary and Elizabeth knew what Joseph himself did not know about the divine pregnancy of the Blessed Virgin Mary and treated him with indescribable reverence. Saint Joseph said how happy he was now that the pain of Mary's absence was over. Most sorrowfully and in tears did Zachary and Elizabeth allow Joseph and Mary to depart for Nazareth. The return journey again took four days and great good was done to certain people

on the way, especially the deliverance of some souls from the snares of Satan.

In the fifth month of the divine pregnancy of the Blessed Virgin Mary, (*See Scriptural accounts below) because of the perfection of Her body and the evidence which became noticeable to Saint Joseph at this time, his heart was wounded with an arrow of grief from which he could not deliver himself.

There were several reasons for this grief. One reason Saint Joseph was especially tormented was that since he so loved and reverenced Mary on account of Her charming graces and incomparable holiness and was bound to Her with his inmost soul, he naturally held a loving desire to have a response of his love from his Spouse. Instead, what

* Scriptural accounts of Our Savior Jesus Christ, Son of God, and His conception by the Holy Ghost in the womb of the Blessed Ever-Virgin Mary.

St. Luke 1

²⁶...the angel Gabriel was sent from God into a city of Galilee called Nazareth,

²⁷To a virgin espoused to a man whose name was Joseph, of the house of David; and the virgin's name was Mary.

²⁸And the angel, being come in, said unto her: Hail, full of grace, the Lord is with thee; blessed art thou among women.

²⁹Who, having heard, was troubled at his saying and thought with herself what manner of salutation this should be.

³⁰And the angel said to her: Fear not, Mary, for thou hast found grace with God.

³¹Behold, thou shalt conceive in thy womb and shalt bring forth a son: and thou shalt call his name JESUS.

³²He shall be great and shall be called the Son of the Most High. And the Lord God shall give unto him the throne of David his father; and he shall reign in the house of Jacob for ever.

³³And of his kingdom there shall be no end.

³⁴And Mary said to the angel: How shall this be done, because I know not man?

³⁵And the angel, answering, said to her: The Holy Ghost shall come upon thee and the power of the Most High shall overshadow thee. And therefore also the Holy which shall be born of thee shall be called the Son of God.

³⁶And, behold, thy cousin Elizabeth, she also hath conceived a son in her old age; and this is the sixth month with her that is called barren.

³⁷Because no word shall be impossible with God.

³⁸And Mary said: Behold the handmaid of the Lord; be it done to me according to thy word. And the angel departed from her.

St. Matthew 1

¹⁸Now the generation of Christ was in this wise. When his mother Mary was espoused to Joseph, before they came together, she was found with child, of the Holy Ghost.

¹⁹Whereupon Joseph her husband, being a just man and not willing publicly to expose her, was minded to put her away privately.

²⁰But while he thought on these things, behold, the angel of the Lord appeared to him in his sleep, saying: Joseph, son of David, fear not to take unto thee Mary thy wife, for that which is conceived in her is of the Holy Ghost

²¹And she shall bring forth a son; and thou shalt call his name JESUS: for he shall save his people from their sins.

²²Now all this was done that it might be fulfilled which the Lord spoke by the prophet, saying:

²³Behold, a virgin shall be with child and bring forth a son; and they shall call his name EMMANUEL, which, being interpreted is, God with us.

²⁴And Joseph rising up from sleep did as the angel of the Lord had commanded him and took unto him his wife,

²⁵And he knew her not till she brought forth her firstborn son; and he called his name JESUS.

he beheld now seemed to tempt poor Joseph to believe un-faithfulness was present. But Joseph never allowed the clear evidence to take his judgment beyond what he saw. He held all judgment. If he had believed any guilt to be present he would surely have died of grief.

Another reason for his grief was the torment of public dishonor when things became known. Also, and most intimate, was the dread of being obliged to hand over his Spouse to the authorities for stoning. His grief therefore, kept to himself, caused him to be surrounded with the sorrows of death. He tried to find a solution in solitude but grief suspended his faculties. He simply could not break his trust in Mary. He could not link sin with Her, yet he could not find any solution. He turned to God and after speaking of the entire matter, ended thus: "I withhold and deny judgment. Not being able to penetrate to the cause of what I see, I pour out in Thy presence my afflicted soul, God of Abraham, Isaac and Jacob. Receive my tears as an acceptable sacrifice; and if my sins merit Thy indignation, let Thy own clemency and kindness move Thee not to despise my excruciating sorrow. Govern Thou my mind and heart by Thy divine light, in order that I may know and fulfill that which is most pleasing to Thee." Many more loving petitions Saint Joseph persevered in. At times he was so pressed with the force of the evidence that he was cast on waves of doubt, and from sheer exhaustion could find neither certainty nor peace. Yet his forbearance in this torment was proven very great.

All this time Mary said nothing of Her secret but waited even more lovingly on Joseph. Saint Joseph himself said nothing of his torments although Mary knew the state of his

soul. Her closeness in serving him and the increasing evidence only tormented him the more. Mary could have proven Her innocence by testimony from Zachary and Elizabeth. But She did nothing of the kind, waiting on a sign from the Lord and trusting in Him.

Carried away by grief, the Saint could not always hide his cruel sorrow and sometimes even spoke with some degree of severity to his Spouse. He did this not in anger, which never entered his thoughts, but only from the natural affliction of his heart.

God seemed not to hear their prayers, leaving themselves in the dark as to the solution. In this way He allowed them to practice faith, hope and love, humility, patience, peace in heroic degree, thereby giving them an opportunity to merit an increase in glory and furnish us an example.

In time, the sure conviction of Mary's pregnancy coupled with Her ever-increasing health, charm and loveliness so afflicted and confused Joseph that he was finally stranded on the shores of grief. He became broken in body, his strength vanished away as his interior anxiety and torment acted upon him. All this became visible and quite incurable since he sought comfort in no one.

Of course Mary suffered greatly in Her compassion for him. Yet She did every possible thing to relieve his misery except reveal Her secret. Thereupon Saint Joseph arrived at this conclusion after the following agonizing struggle: "Is it possible that a Woman of such habits, and in whom such graces of the Lord are manifest, can bring over me such affliction? How can this prudence and holiness agree with these open signs of Her infidelity to God and to me, who love Her so much? If I conclude to send Her away, or to leave Her, I lose Her most loving company, all my comfort, my home and my tranquility. What blessing equal to Her can I find if I withdraw from Her? What consolation, if this one fails? But all this weighs less than the infamy connected with this sad misfortune, and that I should come to be looked upon as Her accomplice in crime. That this event remain concealed is not possible since time will reveal all, even if I strive now to hide it. To pass as the author of this pregnancy will be vile deceit and a blotch on my good name and conscience. I cannot recognize it as caused by me, nor can I ascribe it to any other source known to me. Hence, what am I to do in this dire stress? The least evil will be to absent myself and leave my house before Her delivery comes upon Her; for then I would be still more confused and afflicted. I would then be obliged to live in my own house with a child not my own, without being able to find any outlet or expedient."

Most holy Mary, knowing of Joseph's decision, pleaded with God to come to his aid and deliver him from his affliction.

God immediately allowed angels to inspire Joseph with peace, trust and other inspirations which lasted a short while.

Thereupon Mary pleaded with Her unborn holy Son to keep Joseph from leaving Her. The most High answered that the time was nigh that Joseph would learn the great sacrament that he was actually custodian of.

In the meantime Saint Joseph resolved to depart that night. He packed some clothes and trifles and a little wages he had earned, and prepared to retire. How ever, because of his unusual undertaking, he first commended his intentions to God in prayer: he ex plained what he was doing and why, and said he would henceforth live in the desert and begged God not to forsake him.

At this point, by the secret ordination of God, both Saint Joseph and the Blessed Virgin Mary had reached the utmost sorrow, thereby meriting much and deserving the coming blessings and consolations.

At this time, while asleep, Saint Joseph was visited by the Archangel Gabriel. Gabriel spoke interiorly to Joseph and the Saint understood now the great Mystery that had taken place: the Incarnation. The angel spoke to Joseph in his sleep because, for one reason, his afflicted and disturbed senses were unfit to receive the angel's message without the rest and peace obtained in sleep. That is why so often in the Old Testament, when they had not the New Law of grace and the purification of the senses by the sacraments, angels spoke to men in sleep. Even today in the "dream of the night" which may be compared to the conflicts with the power of darkness and the battle of temptations, we may hear the voice of the Lord through inspirations and the ministry of the angels as did Saint Joseph.

Saint Joseph awoke with the full knowledge that his Spouse was the true Mother of God. He was at once full of joy, and yet sorrow, too, when he realized all he had put Mary through. He blamed himself for all that he felt he should have done concerning most holy Mary and Her high condition and office. He resolved to throw himself before Her and ask Her pardon. He waited till She would come from Her room. In the meantime he unwrapped the small bundle which he had prepared, shedding many tears with feelings quite different from those with which he had made it up. Weeping, he began to show his reverence for his heavenly Spouse, by setting the rooms in order, scrubbing the floors, which were to be touched by the sacred feet of Mary. He resolved to henceforth be Her servant. The blessed Virgin Mary knew all he did and awaited him with sweetest kindness and mildness.

Saint Joseph threw himself upon his knees, begging pardon from Mary in that he had presumed to leave Her and had treated Her as inferior instead of as Mother of God. He asked Her to remember that he did all in ignorance; however, he would not rise till he obtained Her pardon and blessing.

Of course Mary sweetly consoled Her Spouse and explained why She could not reveal Her secret. At this time Saint Joseph saw by special enlightenment the great dignity of the Blessed Virgin Mary and also the full understanding of the mysteries of the Incarnation. Moreover our Lord raised him to the high state of sanctity most befitting his dignity as foster-father.

Since Joseph was embarrassed in letting Mary serve him and even tried to do the housework for Her while She was in contemplation, Mary asked God to let Joseph know She desired to do all the humble tasks possible. As the virtue of humility makes all prayers effective and inclines the immutable Being of God to clemency, He heard Her petition and ordered the angel guardian of the blessed Joseph to

instruct him as follows: "Do not frustrate the humble desires of Her who is supreme over all the creatures of heaven and earth. Exteriorly allow Her to serve thee and interiorly treat Her with highest reverence, and at all times and in all places worship the Incarnate Word. It is His will, equally with that of the heavenly Mother, to serve and not to be served, in order to teach the world the knowledge of life and the excellence of humility. In some of the work thou canst assist Her, but always reverence in Her the Lord of all creation."

Thus in this spirit Joseph allowed Mary to serve him. Yet whereas before he seldom visited Mary in Her room, now that he knew Her true dignity he often went there seeking to wait on Her. Joseph slept in one room and worked in another, and Mary occupied the third room of their little house.

In time the Blessed Virgin spoke of preparing little clothes for the birth of Her holy Son. Saint Joseph yearned to give the Infant the richest in the world. As both prayed to know how to treat the Babe when He was born, God informed them: "I have come from heaven to the earth in order to exalt humility and discredit pride, to honor poverty and contemn riches, to destroy vanity and establish truth, and in order to enhance worthily the value of labor. Therefore it is My will that exteriorly you treat Me according to the humble position which I have assumed, as if I were the natural child of both of you, and that interiorly you acknowledge Me as the Son of My Eternal Father, and bestow the reverence and love due to Me as the Man-God."

So while the Blessed Virgin Mary and Saint Joseph furnished simple, poor exterior apparel for the divine Infant, according to God's desires concerning holy poverty, they likewise furnished the Infant with unspeakable interior riches by way of prayer and devotion. This should be a lesson to all who handle sacred objects in the service of the Lord even as Joseph and Mary handled the Infant's clothes. Great attention, reverence and devotion should accompany such acts. This would truly be worshiping in "spirit and truth."

It was decreed by Almighty God that the Savior be born in Bethlehem. God worked this by allowing Joseph to be called from Nazareth to Bethlehem by order of the Roman Empire in its edict concerning the census which would enable Rome to tax everyone.

Upon hearing the edict, Joseph returned home in sorrowful consternation and told Mary all. The Blessed Virgin told him not to worry as nothing happened to them unless God allowed it, and to resign themselves to His will.

Poor Saint Joseph did not want to part from Mary and make the trip alone, yet neither did he want to take Her who was so close to giving birth to the Infant Jesus, especially when his poverty would find it impossible to provide suitably for Mary on the journey. He asked the Blessed Virgin to ask God to somehow arrange things so that he would not be separated from Her.

God answered that the Blessed Virgin Mary should accompany Joseph, and that though their sufferings would be great, His powerful arms would bring them forth gloriously from all their afflictions. She told Joseph, and he was delighted that he would have Her company. He mistakenly relied on finding the necessary aid from relatives in Bethlehem.

The journey would last five days. After some difficulty in finding a little beast of burden, and leaving their house in the care of a neighbor, the couple set out with a few provisions. The journey was all the more difficult because it was midwinter. Joseph anxiously sought in every way to please and comfort Mary and She in turn inspired him to bear all with courage, patience and joy for love of God; Poor

and humble in the eyes of the world, yet with invisible ac-
companiment of angels, most holy Mary and Saint Joseph
left Nazareth.

Although they received favors on their journey, they also received many rude, annoying and disagreeable encounters, especially in the taverns where many others, because of the edict, were stopping over. They were counted for little because of their modest dress and behavior.

Most Holy Mary suffered much from the journey, most of all because She knew the state of the souls of the many different people She met on the way and some She knew were reprobate. Knowing this and praying for all others according to their different needs caused Her much sorrow and taxed the strength of Her body, even more than the traveling. Moreover the wintry weather caused further hardships (although Mary had the power to control the weather, but did not do so for Her own relief). Faithful Joseph however did his utmost to help Her and shield Her.

In Bethlehem Mary silently bore with Joseph while he sorrowfully found house after house and heart after heart, even of relatives, closed to them. She knew this would happen yet patiently bore all in obedience to Joseph without the slightest complaint.

Heartbroken, Saint Joseph finally was forced to lead Mary to a deserted cave outside town. Sweetest Mary consoled Joseph, saying it was the Lord's will and they could make Him happy by joyfully accepting this chance to practice poverty which is so pleasing to Him since poverty was man's shortest and surest way for reaching the heights of divine love and union with God.

This cave was held in such contempt by people that though the town was full of strangers none would degrade himself by making use of it. But the eternal Father had reserved it for the Holy Family, consecrating it in all its barrenness, loneliness and poverty as the first temple of light and as the house of the true Sun of Justice, which was to arise from the resplendent Aurora Mary for the upright of heart, turning the night of sin into the daylight of grace.

The brightness of the angels enabled the holy pair to see the interior of the barren cave. Mary and Joseph thereupon thanked and praised God for saving this place for them. They asked God to bless all who turned them away thus enabling them to come to this place of such great favors. Considering this place now to be the temple of the Lord, they set about cleaning it and later Joseph made a fire, as it was bitter cold, and they ate their frugal supper in joy.

As Mary felt the approach of the blessed Birth She besought Joseph to take his rest. First Joseph made a sort of couch for Mary, using the manger and some of their wearing apparel. After this Joseph began his prayers and, by God's design, was wrapt in ecstasy till after the Divine Birth.

Then took place very great and profound mysteries and favors concerning the most Blessed Virgin Mary and the birth of Her divine Son. Joyfully and miraculously She gave birth to the Infant Savior and Redeemer. Saint Michael and Saint Gabriel were Her assistants in this birth. Most sacred canticles, and words full of hidden mysteries took place now between Mary and Her new-born Son. The angels too, sang canticles.

Now it was time to call Saint Joseph who had all the while been informed of these mysteries in his ecstasy. It was

only right that he should behold his Savior before any other mortal. He adored Him in profoundest humility and in tears of joy. While Mary held the Infant, Joseph handed Her the swaddling-clothes. Then the divine Babe was laid in the manger and animals came up and warmed Him with their breath. Thus was fulfilled the prophecy, that "the ox knoweth his owner, and the ass his master's crib; but Israel hath not known Me, and My people hath not understood."

One note by our most Holy Mother might be remembered here: "Learn from my example the reverence, fear and respect, with which thou must treat Him, remembering how I acted, when I held Him in my arms; follow my example, whenever thou receivest Him in thy heart in the venerable sacrament of the Holy Eucharist, wherein is contained the same God-Man, Who was born of my womb. In this holy Sacrament thou receivest Him and possessest Him just as really, and He remains in thee just as actually, as I possessed Him and conversed with Him, although in another manner. I desire that thou go even to extremes in this holy reverence and fear; and I wish that thou take notice and be convinced, that in entering into thy heart in the holy Sacrament, thy God exhorts thee in the same words, as spoken to me: 'become like unto Me.'"

The first visitors chosen to witness this greatest of God's works, and to see Mary and Joseph and the Infant lying in the manger, were not the rich nor the powerful, but simple, ignorant shepherds. These understood and adored and were raised to a new state of grace and holiness. They brought what presents their poverty allowed during the days the Holy Family remained there.

ost holy Mary sometimes asked Saint Joseph to hold the divine Infant in order to give him joy. Saint Joseph's desire to hold the Infant God and his reverential fear caused him to make heroic acts of love, faith, humility and profoundest reverence. Trembling with discreet fear he fell on his knees to receive Him from the hands of His most holy Mother, while sweetest tears of joy and delight copiously flowed from his eyes at happiness so extraordinary.

In due time the rite of Circumcision had to be reckoned with. Was Her divine Son to submit to this law, Mary wanted to know of God? Although God informed Her of His will, saying that this was only one of many sufferings in the path of His Only-begotten Son, Mary conferred with Joseph who wisely and modestly said that it would be best to follow the Law since their Son wanted in all things to conform to the divine will manifested in the Law.

Since both Joseph and Mary had been informed by angels from the beginning that their Infant was to be called Jesus, they agreed to tell the performing priest that this was the chosen name. When the priest arrived, he was a bit astonished by the rude dwelling at first, but at the presence of the holy couple his attitude was changed to devotion. Most holy Mary was soon to become the first altar upon which our Savior would shed His first drop of Blood. Saint Joseph was the first, silent, prayerful witness to celebrate in a divine Sacrifice besides the holy Mother.

Saint Joseph was not at the Sacrifice of Calvary with Mary but he joined with Her in this one with perfect devotion.

Some time after the Circumcision the angels announced that the three Wise Men, or kings, were on their way to worship the new-born King. Since Joseph was going to remain in Bethlehem till the Presentation; he now waited for the kings to arrive. Meanwhile he and Mary did all they could to make the cave a more fitting place to live.

Saint Joseph remained at the Blessed Virgin's side when the kings arrived to adore the Infant Jesus. It was not necessary that he go away because the kings had already been instructed that the Mother of the Newborn was a Virgin and that He was the true God and not a son of Saint Joseph. After praising and worshiping our Savior and His mysteries,

and conversing with the Blessed Virgin, the kings congratulated Saint Joseph on his good fortune. Before leaving, the three kings left other gifts, besides the gold, frankincense and myrrh, which Joseph and Mary distributed to the poor.

After many various and wonderful events having taken place in this cave of Christmas blessings, Joseph and Mary accepted a poor and pious woman's offer of living in her home till the time of the Purification and Presentation. While living with the woman, most holy Mary was visited by different people, mostly of the poorest class, whom She instructed in the faith and the truth about the Messias (without telling them who She was). Sometimes their talk about these matters was so full of error and womanish prattle, the simple Saint Joseph smiled in secret. He marveled at the wisdom, patience and gentleness of the Blessed Mother Mary in teaching all that was good for them to know.

Joseph and Mary took leave of this good woman with whom they had lived, in order to get to Jerusalem in time for the Presentation, forty days after the Divine Birth. Mary knew the Savior wished to offer Himself as a living Victim to the Eternal Father in thanksgiving for having formed His most pure body and created His most holy Soul; for having destined Him as an acceptable Sacrifice for the human race and for the welfare of mortals, all in conformity to the divine will.

The blessed Virgin wanted to make the journey on foot, and barefoot at that, but having asked Joseph, he said the weather would not allow Her to go bare foot. Mary humbly and obediently obeyed even though She knew the wonderful composition of Her body enabled Her to bear such a penance. The Holy Family thus departed for Jerusalem with the clothes of the Infant and the gifts of the kings to be used in the temple offering, all carried upon their little beast of burden. On this journey the weather was unusually severe and again the Holy Mother made use of Her power to keep the elements from Her Son all the while bearing the suffering Herself.

Simeon, the priest of the temple, and Anna, the Prophetess, were enlightened by the Holy Ghost as to the coming of the Incarnate Word and the poverty of the holy couple bringing Him. Therefore they procured a place for them to

stay beforehand. Saint Joseph brought the gifts of the kings to the temple when there were not a lot of people around and did not even tell the one who received the gifts that he was the donor of these presents, thus avoiding all ostentation and vanity ill-befitting a true man of poverty.

This law of presenting the first-born son in the temple was the will of God and was carried out by the men of the Old Testament with the hope that one of these first born would be the Messias. Mary knew the will and desires of the Heavenly Father and of Her Divine Son and She answered the Father with a most loving prayer: "... If Thou hast given

Him to me as a God, I return Him to Thee as God and Man; His value is infinite ..."

The next morning the little Infant, resting in the arms of Mary, went to the temple. Saint Joseph, with the two turtle doves and candles, accompanied them. It was at this time that the holy priest Simeon pronounced these famous and mysterious words "Now Thou dost dismiss Thy servant, O Lord, in peace. Because my eyes have seen Thy salvation, which Thou hast prepared before the face of all peoples: a light for the revelation of the gentiles, and the glory of Thy people Israel."

Then also Simeon said that to which the little Infant bowed His head in obedience and to which His Holy Mother began to feel as a sword of sorrow piercing Her heart: "Behold this Child is set for the fall and for the resurrection of many in Israel, and for a sign which shall be contradicted. And thy own soul a sword shall pierce, that out of many hearts thoughts may be revealed." Saint Joseph was given to understand much of these mysteries but not so much as the Virgin Mother because he was to serve a different purpose, and furthermore was not going to live to see the Passion.

The most holy Mary kissed the hand of the priest and that of Her former teacher in the temple, Anne the Prophetess, after the ceremony was over. Then She departed with Saint Joseph.

In the mystery of the Presentation we learn these lessons: As our Lord offered Himself in readiness for the perfect Sacrifice and His holy Mother and guardian Saint Joseph offered themselves in their roles as His helpers, so we should not offer ourselves in mere sentiment and in empty words, of oft-repeated exclamations of: "Lord, Lord," and, when the occasion of tasting the chalice and the cross of suffering is at hand, turn away in sorrow and affliction from the sufferings by which the sincerity of a loving and affectionate heart is to be tried. When trial comes upon us we should fervently exclaim: "The Lord is my light and my salvation, whom shall I fear?" We must bear our sorrows calmly, remaining in peace, as did Mary and Joseph when Simeon prophesied his warning.

After five more days in Jerusalem God revealed that Mary was to flee with Her Son and Saint Joseph to Egypt on a very trying journey since the murderous Herod was seeking them. Joseph and Mary knew that God could annihilate Herod in an instant, but they also knew that Christ and His followers were to be persecuted till the end of time and that we should not always expect miracles of deliverance but rather always obey God even if it means loss of our life. Neither should we have expected God to save the innocent children from Herod, since by their martyrdom they obtained eternal life. Had they been saved by a miracle, some would eventually have lost their souls.

The Infant Jesus wept a little to show He was grateful to Mary and Joseph for their sorrow upon seeing that the men who needed this sweet Savior most were actually seeking to kill Him.

With faith and hope the holy couple left Jerusalem, but with anxiety too, because they knew not what to expect in journeying to a strange land, especially with a Babe only

weeks old. The holy angels however said they would be their guides and the couple were much comforted at this. The angels told Mary not to delay because people were beginning to rumor it about that She was the Mother of the Messias, and Herod had ordered a thorough search. The angels also said that God commanded they flee at night.

Saint Elizabeth, having learned of Herod's treachery from one of Mary's angels, sent a servant to meet the Holy Family in Gaza about twenty hours from Jerusalem. This servant brought some provisions especially for the Infant's needs.

*E*ven on this journey Mary helped all those She could by giving to the poor whatever supplies She didn't need and by healing some sick of body or soul, but they told no one who they were or where they were going.

*W*hen Mary tried to console Her little Infant with sweet prayers, He replied, "All the labors, O Mother, and all fatigue are most light and sweet to Me, since I undergo them for the honor of My eternal Father and for the instruction and Redemption of men, especially in thy company." Nevertheless He wept several times and His holy Mother understood that these tears were caused by His compassion for the salvation of men and by their ingratitude. The fortunate Joseph witnessed these divine mysteries and received much consolation in his anxieties.

*S*omething we must pay attention to here is that the loving, patient, meek Lamb, Jesus, prayed for the very one who was seeking His life. Although Herod was not saved, his punishment was greatly lessened. As did our Lord, we must pray for our enemies. Be sides, those who persecute us do us a great favor since they give us a chance to imitate our Savior and gain merit.

*A*fter leaving the city of Gaza, the pilgrims entered the sandy deserts of Bersabe, which they had to cross before reaching their future home in Heliopolis which is now a suburb of Cairo, Egypt. This desert journey was several days of hard and slow traveling. All suffered much on this journey—Mary in anxiety for Her divine Son and Joseph, and Joseph was deeply grieved not to be able by his efforts and care to ease the hardships of the Child and his Spouse.

All through this desert trip they had only the open sky for shelter—and it was the time of winter— Saint Joseph did the best he could in making a shelter for Jesus and Mary with some sticks and his own cloak. Mary knew that Jesus was offering to the Father Her sufferings and Joseph's also. She united Her acts of worship with His. This is our obligation and blessed opportunity too. Saint Joseph, always caring for Them and ignoring his own comfort, slept on the ground with his head on their chest for clothes and other articles.

In time their food ran short so that they had to beg the assistance of their heavenly Father in order to continue the proper care of their little Child. God did not answer right away but rather also allowed a storm to afflict them which Mary commanded to afflict Her alone. After patient suffering with love and humble prayers, the Holy Family was relieved of both inclement weather and hunger too as the angels came with more than they asked for. We learn from this God always assists us in our needs if we only trust in Him instead of creatures or greedy haste or dishonest ways. Moreover men often seek that which is merely for show to others instead of limiting themselves to what is strictly necessary.

Because of the mysterious plans of God, the Holy Family traveled in a round-about way in the flight into Egypt in order to allow the Infant Savior to visit and sanctify so many hitherto idolatrous places. This trip actually consumed more than fifty days, or more than two hundred leagues.[2] Thus from the arms of His Blessed Mother the Divine Savior routed out and threw down the demons and their idols as He passed from town to town, while Saint Joseph witnessed, marveled and praised God for the divine deliverance of so many inhabitants.

*M*any people in their ignorance and terror at witnessing such events came to the strangers, Joseph and Mary, who in turn took the opportunity to preach the news of salvation to them and teach them to have sorrow for their sins. The principal wonders took place in Heliopolis which, with mysterious fitness, was called the city of the Sun and is now called Cairo, the grand. It was nothing less than love for souls that caused the Holy Family to bear so much otherwise unnecessary labors and journeying in this flight. Lucifer was much enraged to see his kingdom toppling but he did not know that it was this little Infant that was doing it. He had been overcome so many times by the Blessed Virgin's holiness that he now blamed Her for these doings. In truth the most holy Mary did have much to do with the overthrow of the demons and in Her magnificent victories over Satan it is fitting to recall a Psalm She had sung for our imitation. "Who is like to God our Lord; that dwells on high and looks upon the humble in heaven and on earth?"

*S*aint Joseph finally found and bought a poor and humble yet serviceable house at a small distance from Heliopolis. They set about cleaning up the house, and since they were not stranded in the desert, but near people, God did not help them miraculously but allowed them to rely on others and even to beg. The Infant Jesus allowed Himself to come to the need of living by begging in order to repay a hundred-fold those who gave to Saint Joseph as he uncomplainedly went about begging.

As soon as he could, Saint Joseph earned wages by his work. He also made some simple furniture, etc., for the bare house. All through these trying days of poverty in settling in this new land we must recall that Joseph and Mary bore all in joy and peace and regretted not whatever convenience and goods they left in their former home. Yet we Catholics not only do not use the opportunity of being deprived of certain conveniences in order to make up for some of our sins, but complain even to or against God, and also when we do have all our needs filled, never cease feverishly securing ever more luxuries, etc.

Saint Joseph had difficulty as a carpenter to make a suitable living here, so the most Blessed Mary obtained needlework from women who were attracted by Her modesty and sweetness. Her skill soon became well known. Of course Joseph and Mary always trusted in God and united prayer to all their labors. When Mary let Saint Joseph hold the Infant Savior, he would forget all the hardships of his labor and they would seem sweet and easy to him. Do we perform our duties for Him? and offer them to Him? Remember we, as Joseph, can often, even daily, hold Him at Mass in Holy Communion.

Most holy Mary, after our Lord had brought so many idols crashing down, constantly instructed and healed people, but after they had lived there two years, Saint Joseph began to cure the sick and instruct the increasing number of those afflicted in body and soul. Saint Joseph ordinarily taught and cured the men and Mary the women. These holy laborers received many gifts from the people which they gave to the poor, and they continued to live off the earnings of Saint Joseph.

Most holy Mary instructs us here in saying that we need not seek occasions in laboring for the salvation of our neighbors, for the Lord will send them... except in some extraordinary circumstances. But we should seek to exert our influence upon all... not presuming to take upon ourselves the office of a teacher, but of one that seeks to console, and one that pities the hardships of her brothers; as one who with much reserve and humility and with great charity seeks to exhort them to patience. Pray without ceasing for those to whom you cannot speak.

$\mathcal{A}$lthough the Infant Savior spoke with His Virgin Mother right from the time of His birth, it was not till one year had passed since His birth that He spoke His first words to Saint Joseph. One time when Joseph and Mary were speaking of the infinite love of God in sending a Savior, the Infant took the occasion to speak these first words to His foster-father: "My father, I came from heaven upon this earth in order to be the light of the world, and in order to rescue it from darkness of sin; in order to seek and know My sheep as a good Shepherd, to give them nourishment of eternal life, teach them the way of heaven, open its gates, which had been closed by their sins. I desire that you both be children of the Light, which you have so close at hand."

$\mathcal{S}$aint Joseph was overjoyed to hear Our Lord call him "father" in His first words and begged our Lord for the light and grace to fulfill His will entirely.

$\mathcal{W}$hen the first year had passed some other change took place also. Instead of swaddling clothes the Blessed Mother wanted to dress Her Infant in other garments. In our Lord's answer to this we learn much for our own imitation, for He said: "Clothe Me, My Mother, in a tunic of a lowly and ordinary color. This alone will I wear, and it shall grow with Me. Over this garment shall they cast lots at My death; for even this shall not be left at My disposal, but at the disposal of others; so that men shall see that I was born and wish to live poor and destitute of visible things, which being earthly, oppress and darken the heart of man... I shall not have anything to do with visible things except to offer them up to the eternal Father, renouncing them for His love, and making use of only so much as is sufficient to sustain My natural life, which I will afterwards yield up for man's sake. By this example I wish to impress upon the world the doctrine that it must love poverty and not despise it; for I, Who am the Lord of the whole world, entirely repudiated and rejected its possessions. Those who know Me by faith should be filled with confusion at seeing themselves desire what I taught them to despise." Further words reveal other teachings never voiced by the world: "My Mother, I will permit a slight and ordinary covering for My feet until the time of My public preaching shall come, for this I must do barefooted. But I do not wish to wear linen, because it foments carnal pleasures, and is the cause of many vices in men. I wish to teach many by My example to renounce it for love and imitation of Me."

This is why Saint Joseph is a perfect model in the virtue of poverty for all ages: he learned this perfection from the lips of the divine Teacher Himself.

hen Jesus reached the end of His seventh year while in Egypt, Saint Joseph received word by angel at night that the Holy Family should return to Nazareth since Herod was dead. This was a sacrifice because they were well settled—more so than they had been in Nazareth.

God so much values proper order in created things that He did not have Jesus or Mary make the arrangements but rather Saint Joseph who was head of the Holy Family. We learn from this that in the Mystical Body even those of more virtue but less authority should obey their superiors in all that is not sin.

They resolved to leave immediately and distributed the little furniture they had to the poor. As they departed, the people most sorrowfully wept and sighed. If God had not interfered, the Holy Family would have had great difficulty in leaving. As they traveled, they again healed the sick and threw out many devils.

Again they entered the desert and suffered many hardships with great merit. Saint Joseph, upon reaching Palestine, had his sorrows increased when he learned that Archelaus had succeeded his father, Herod, and feared he had inherited his cruelty. Therefore he finally settled in Nazareth. Their little house was still in perfect condition because of the faithful woman with whom they had left it. With utmost thanks to God they began life anew.

Labor, which by other sons of Adam is considered a punishment and hardship, was for Saint Joseph a blessing and consolation knowing that he had been chosen by his labor and sweat to support God Himself and His Mother. We should receive consolation knowing that, as Saint Joseph, we can offer our work to God, doing it for Him.

Besides this consolation there was for Saint Joseph the greatest joy in having the sweetest Mary serve his smallest needs. This was because Saint Joseph bore his duties so faithfully.

Concerning this latest trial of Saint Joseph and Family and their being uprooted from their way of life in Egypt, most holy Mary gives us some instruction on how to act in similar circumstances: "...preserve thy heart independent and riveted only on the divine Providence, without ever allowing it to incline toward what it desires or longs for, or to abhor what is painful to it. Let the will of the Lord be thy only delight and joy. Let neither thy desires draw thee on, nor thy fears dishearten thee. Let not thy exterior occupations, and much less thy regard or attention to creatures, ever impede thee or divert thee from thy holy exercises, attending always to my example."

Soon after arriving in Nazareth, Saint Joseph had to present himself in the temple at Jerusalem since the Jewish men had to do this three times a year. Although the women were not obliged to go, Joseph and Mary decided all would go on this Feast of Unleavened Bread, lasting seven days. (Nazareth to Jerusalem: 30 leagues.[3]) The Child Jesus desired to make the trip on foot and allowed all the natural fatigue of such a trip to afflict Him, already taking on hardships in the service of His Father and for our advantage. Joseph and Mary did all they could to ease the fatigue of their divine Son and they received much joyful reward in certain little things, for instance, very often they observed the wind would flutter through the divine Child's hair as He walked along. Although He worked secretly, our Lord performed many pre-arranged works of charity for the good of souls as they traveled, our Lady was pierced with a sword of sorrow as our Lord revealed to Her the sufferings He would undergo in this very city of Jerusalem which they were now visiting. Thus they both offered these sufferings to the Trinity applying them for the benefit of the faithful.

Now at twelve years the divine Child and His parents made another trip to Jerusalem that has become known so well in the Gospel. It was now time to let the divine splendors shine forth. As before, this journey was made at the time of the Feast of Unleavened Bread. Having performed their acts of devotion, the Holy Family departed for Nazareth.

It was during this departure from Jerusalem that our Lord withdrew from His parents without being noticed. He could do this more easily since it was the custom for the women to travel in a group separate from the men. Saint Joseph of course reckoned Jesus was, as always, with His most Blessed Mother. But with Mary it was not so easy to withdraw from unnoticed, therefore God so diverted Her with holy thoughts and contemplation that She did not notice Jesus' absence immediately. When She did notice, She supposed He was with Saint Joseph. An entire day slipped by before Joseph and Mary met and were struck dumb with amazement and surprise when they realized His disappearance.

*B*oth blamed themselves and after some time tried to decide how best to locate Him since they could never rest till they did.

*F*irst seeking Him among friends and relatives (as so often we do) they received answers which only in creased their anxiety since none had seen Him. The Blessed Virgin's angels could have revealed the secret to Her as She lovingly and sorrowfully complained to them, but by their evasive answers the most humble Mary knew God did not wish to enlighten Her further and thus Her grief increased. She thought possibly Archelaus (son of Herod) had found Him and though it was not His hour for death He may be under going some mistreatment. Another possibility which tormented Her was that Her conduct had somehow displeased Him and perhaps He had gone to the desert to live with Saint John the Baptist.

*W*ithout ceasing, therefore, and without sleeping or eating, the great Queen sought Her treasure. This was one of Mary's greatest sorrows since She was not certain why Her beloved Son had left Her nor how She would again find Him, yet She bore Herself magnificently, not losing Her interior peace, all the while trusting in God and reverencing and praising Him.

During these three days our Mother was encouraged when different women informed Her they had seen Her gracious, beautiful Son on different errands of mercy and consolation to the poor and sick. Still not finding Him, however, She knew one other place He would certainly visit: the temple of His heavenly Father. Her angels now encouraged Her to go there as Her sorrowful search was coming to an end.

It was at this time that the glorious patriarch Saint Joseph met his spouse, for they had separated in order to increase the chances of finding the divine Child. During all these days Saint Joseph had suffered unspeakable sorrow and affliction, hastening from one place to another. He was in serious danger of losing his life during this time, if the hand of the Lord had not strengthened him and if the most prudent Lady had not consoled him and forced him to take some food and rest. His sincere and exquisite love for the divine Child made him so anxious and solicitous to find Him, that he would have allowed himself no time or care to take nourishment for the support of nature.

Following the advice of the angels, most holy Mary and Joseph betook themselves to the temple.

In connection with this sorrow of Joseph and Mary, our Mother teaches us this wisdom: "I was deprived of the bodily presence of my most holy Son: but although I was in hope of again finding Him, yet, in my great love, the uncertainty as to the cause of His withdrawal gave me no rest until I found Him. In this I wish that thou imitate me, whether thou lose Him through thy own fault or by the disposition of His own will. So great should be thy dread of losing Him through thy fault, that neither tribulation, nor trouble, nor necessity, nor danger, nor persecution, nor the sword, neither height nor depth should ever withhold thee from seeking after thy God (Rom. 8:35); for if thou art faithful as thou shouldst be, and if thou dost not wish to lose Him, neither the angels, nor the principalities, nor the powers, nor any other creature can ever deprive thee of Him. So strong are the bonds of His love and its chains, that no one can burst them, except thy own free will."

It was at this temple to which Joseph and Mary hastened that the divine Child Jesus, after having performed many marvelous works of grace and nature upon the people of Jerusalem, mingled with certain distinguished men who were discussing whether or not the Messias had come into the world. After the majority, who believed wrongly in a coarse interpretation of a worldly, temporal ruler, argued into silence the few who believed in the true Messias of an eternal, spiritual kingdom—after this the Child Jesus, the Teacher of Truth, Who could not let error prevail, stepped into their midst with exceeding majesty and grace, as one who would propose some doubt of solution. By His pleasing appearance He awakened in the hearts of these learned men a desire to hear Him attentively. He proceeded with marvelous wisdom to prove from the Scriptures that the Messias had come and that He would set up a spiritual kingdom.

The teachers were dumbfounded but did not suspect that He was Himself the Messias. It was at this time that Joseph and Mary arrived, hearing Him speak His last arguments. Absorbed in joy, the heavenly Lady approached and asked that recorded question: "Son, why hast Thou done so to us? Behold Thy father and I have sought Thee sorrowing." This loving complaint was uttered with equal reverence and affection, adoring Him as God and manifesting Her maternal affliction.

When our Lord answered: "Why is it that you sought Me? Did you not know that I must be about My Father's business?" it was because the full meaning of His words were not understood by Joseph and Mary at that time, one reason being the interior joy that now so filled their faculties; another reason being that the time for the full comprehension of what had just been treated of in this discussion with the doctors had not yet arrived for them.

When the learned men departed, Mary embraced Her Son. The divine Child received Her with pleasure. And later some distance from Jerusalem, His most holy Mother fell on Her knees and adored Him. With loving tenderness He raised Her from the ground and comforted Her. It was at this time that all Jesus had spoken of concerning the Messias became clearly revealed to Mary. Moreover He told Her that the doctors had not recognized Him as the Messias because they were inflated and arrogant in their own knowledge.

Arriving in Nazareth the divine Child subjected Himself to Joseph and Mary. In practicing Her role of motherhood, the graces necessary for such ministry and office were given to Her in such abundance, that they overflowed into the soul of Saint Joseph, making him worthy of being the reputed father of Jesus and the head of this family.

Concerning the mystery of this Finding of our Lord in the Temple, our Mother enlightens us with these words: "The Lord absented Himself from me (and Saint Joseph, too) in order that, seeking Him in sorrow and tears, I might find Him again in joy and with abundant fruits for my soul. I desire that thou imitate me in this mystery and seek Him with such earnestness, as to be consumed with a continual longing without ever in thy whole life coming to any rest until thou holdest Him and canst lose Him no more. In order that thou mayest understand better this sacrament of the Lord, remember that the Infinite Wisdom made men capable of His eternal felicity and placed them on the way to this happiness, but left them in doubt of its attainment, as long as they have not yet acquired it, and thus filled them with joyful hope and sorrowful fear of its final acquisition. This anxiety engenders in men a lifelong fear and abhorrence of sin, by which alone they can be deprived of beatitude, and thus prevents them from being ensnared and misled by the corporeal and visible things of this earth. This anxiety the Creator assists by adding to the natural reasoning powers, faith and hope, which are the spurs of their love toward seeking and finding their last end. Besides these virtues and others infused at Baptism, He sends His inspirations and helps to keep awake the soul in the absence of its Lord and to prevent forgetfulness of Him and of itself while deprived of His amiable presence. Thus it pursues the right course until it finds the great goal, where all its inclinations and longing shall be satiated.

LAST DAYS OF
Saint Joseph

When our Lord reached about eighteen years and our Lady thirty-three, Saint Joseph was over fifty years and much broken and worn out as far as his body was concerned. His continual cares, his journeys and his incessant labors for the sustenance of his Spouse and of the Lord had weakened him much more than his years. This was so ordained by the Lord, Who, wishing to lead him on to the practice of patience and of other virtues, permitted him to suffer sickness and pain. His most prudent Spouse, knowing that he was much weakened and always having loved and served him better than any wife ever did her husband, spoke to him and said: "My spouse and my master, I am deeply obliged to you for the faithful labors, watchfulness and care thou hast bestowed on my welfare. For in the sweat of thy brow thou hast until now supported me, thy servant, and my most holy Son, the true God, and in this thy solicitude, thou hast spent thy strength and the best part of thy health and of thy life in protecting me and attending upon my welfare. From the hands of the Almighty thou shalt receive the reward of thy works and the blessings of sweetness which thou deservest. But now I beseech thee, my master, rest henceforth from thy labors since thy impaired strength is not any more equal to them. I wish from now on to show my gratitude by laboring in thy service and provide for such sustenance as the Lord wishes us to have."

The saint listened to the words of his sweetest Spouse with abundant tears of humblest acknowledgment and consolation. Although he at first earnestly entreated Her to be allowed to continue forever in his labors, yet at last he yielded to Her request and obeyed his Spouse, the Mistress of the world. From that time on he rested from the hard labor of his hands, by which he had earned a livelihood for all Three. They gave away the carpenter tools as an alms, not wishing to have anything superfluous or useless in their house and family. Being thus at leisure, Saint Joseph occupied himself entirely in the contemplation of the mysteries of which he was the guardian and in the exercise of virtues. As he had the happiness and good fortune of continually enjoying the sight and the intercourse of the divine Wisdom Incarnate, and of Her, who was the Mother of It, this man of God reached such a height of sanctity that, his heavenly Spouse excepted, no one ever surpassed him and he far outstripped all other creatures. The blessed Lady, and also Her most holy Son, attended upon him and

nursed him in his sickness, consoling and sustaining him with the greatest assiduity; and hence there are no words sufficiently expressive of the humility, reverence and love which all this caused in the simple and grateful heart of this man of God. He thus became the admiration and joy of the angels and the pleasure and delight of the Most High.

*H*enceforth the Mistress of the world took upon Her self the task of supporting by Her work Her most holy Son and Her husband, for such was the will of the eternal Wisdom in order to raise Mary to the very pinnacle of all virtues and perfections and in order to furnish an example for the confusion of the daughters and the sons of Adam and Eve.

*G*od of course could have provided miraculously for the Holy Family but He desired it this way for our instruction and our Lady's glory.

A common defect in all of us that are called to the light and to the profession of holy faith in the school of Christ, our Lord, is that of looking upon Him too much as our Redeemer and not sufficiently as our Teacher in our sufferings. We all desire to reap the fruit of salvation and enter the portals of grace and glory; but we do not with like zeal seek to follow Him on the way of the Cross by which He entered and upon which He invites us to attain eternal glory. Although, as Catholics, we do not fall into such insane errors as the heretics; for we know and profess that without exertion and labor there can be no reward or crown; and that it is a sacrilegious blasphemy to avail oneself of the salvation of Christ in order to sin without remorse or restraint. Nevertheless, as far as really practicing the works inculcated

by faith, some of the children of the Church differ little from the children of darkness; for they look upon difficult and painful works as unnecessary for the following of Christ and for participation in His glory.

Let us throw off this error in our practice and let us understand well that suffering was not only for Christ, our Lord, but also for us; that if He suffered labors and death as the Redeemer of the World, He suffered them also as our Teacher, thereby inviting us as His friends to enter upon the way of His Cross; so much so, that His nearest friends receive the greatest share of suffering, and no one can merit heaven with out the price of personal exertions. In imitation of His most holy Mother, the Apostles, Martyrs, Confessors and Virgins and all His followers have won their crown by labors and those that have been most prepared for suffering have obtained so much the more abundant reward and the higher crown. It might be objected that our Lord was at the same time God and Man, and that if He has given us the most conspicuous and wonderful example of suffering, He did it more in order to be admired than to be imitated.

*B*ut this is only a bold and daring pretense on our part; for He can meet this objection with the example of His Mother, our most pure and innocent Queen, with that of Her blessed spouse, and of so many men and women, weak and deficient as ourselves, who were less guilty, but who have imitated Him and followed Him on the way of the Cross. The Lord did not suffer only in order to excite our admiration, but in order that we imitate His example, and He did not let even His Divinity stand in the way of labor and suffering, but allowed sorrow and suffering to overwhelm Him in proportion to His innocence and sinlessness.

*A*long this royal highway of the Cross the Lord led the spouse of His Blessed Mother, Saint Joseph, whom He loved above all the sons of men. In order to increase his merits and crown before the time of his meriting should come to an end, He visited him in the last years of his life with certain sicknesses, such as fever, violent headaches and very painful rheumatisms, which greatly afflicted and weakened him. In the midst of these infirmities, he was suffering from another source, more sweet, but extremely painful, namely, from the fire of his ardent love which was so vehement, that the flights and ecstasies of his most pure soul would often have burst the bounds of his body if the Lord, Who vouchsafed them, had not strengthened and comforted him against these agonies of love. In these sweet excesses the Lord allowed him to suffer until his death and on account of the natural weakness of his extenuated body, this exercise was the source of ineffable merits for the fortunate saint, not only because of the sufferings occasioned, but because of the love by which these sufferings were brought about.

Our great Queen, his Spouse, was a witness to all these mysteries; She knew the whole interior of the soul of Saint Joseph, being thus rejoiced by the knowledge of having for Her spouse a man so holy and so beloved of the Lord. She beheld and comprehended the sincerity and purity of his soul; his burning love; his exalted and heavenly thoughts; his dove-like patience and meekness in his grievous ailments and exquisite sufferings. She knew that he never complained either of these nor of any of the other trials, nor ever asked for any relief in his wants and necessities; for he bore all with incomparable equanimity and greatness of soul. As his most prudent Spouse contemplated and weighed all these heroic virtues of Saint Joseph, She grew to look upon him with such a veneration as cannot ever be properly estimated by anyone. She labored with incredible joy for his support and comfort; and the greatest of his comforts was that She should prepare and administer his victuals with Her own virginal hand. But as all Her service seemed little in the eyes of the heavenly Lady compared to the necessities of Her spouse, She sometimes, in Her love for him, made use of Her power as Queen and Mistress of all creation and commanded that the food which She administered to him impart special strength and supply new life to this holy and just man of God.

This command of the great Lady, whom all creatures obeyed, was fulfilled; and when Saint Joseph tasted of the victuals, which bore these blessings of sweetness, and when he perceived their effects, he was wont to say to the Queen: "My Lady and Spouse, what celestial food is this which vivifies me, rejoices my senses, restores my strength and fills my soul and spirit with new delight?" The Empress of heaven served him his meals on bended knees; and when he was much disabled and suffering, She took off his shoes in the same posture. At other times She supported him in Her arms. Although the humble saint sought to rouse himself in order to forestall some of these ministrations of his Spouse, he could not altogether prevent them, for She was intimately aware of all his sufferings and weaknesses and of the circumstances and occasions when he needed Her assistance. At such times the heavenly Nurse always hastened to assist him in his wants. Often also, as the Mistress of wisdom and of virtue, She comforted him by words of sweetest consolation. In the last three years of his life, when his infirmities increased, our Queen attended upon him day and night and Her only other employment was the service and ministration due to Her most holy Son. Jesus sometimes joined and assisted Her in the care of Her holy spouse whenever He was not engaged in other necessary works. There was never a sick person, nor will there ever be one, who was so well nursed and comforted. Great was the happiness and worth of this man of God, Saint Joseph, for he alone deserved to have for his Spouse Her, who was the Spouse of the Holy Ghost.

Concerning this part of Saint Joseph's life, our Lady teaches: "One of the virtuous works most pleasing to the Lord and most fruitful for souls, is the loving care of the sick. By it is fulfilled to a great extent that natural law which requires us to do to our neighbors what we wish them to do to us.

In the Gospel this is adduced as one of the works for which the Lord shall give eternal reward to the just (Matt. 25: 34); and the failure to exercise this duty is alleged as one of the causes of the eternal damnation of the wicked. In the same place the justice of this retribution is also explained; namely, as men are the children of the eternal Father, the Lord accounts any good or ill done to our neighbor as done to His own children, whose part He takes; for so it is customary among human parents."

Already eight years Saint Joseph had been exercised by his infirmities and sufferings, and his noble soul had been purified more and more each day in the crucible of affliction and of divine love. As the time passed, his bodily strength gradually diminished and he approached the unavoidable end, in which the stipend of death is paid by all of us children of Adam. In like manner also increased the care and solicitude of his heavenly Spouse, our Queen, assisting and serving him with unbroken punctuality. Perceiving, in Her exalted wisdom, that the day and hour for his departure from this cumbrous earth was very near, the loving Lady betook Herself to Her blessed Son and said to Him: "Lord God Most High, Son of the Eternal Father and Savior of the world, by Thy divine light I see the hour approaching which Thou hast decreed for the death of Thy servant Joseph. I beseech Thee, by Thy ancient mercies and by Thy infinite bounty, to assist him in that hour by Thy almighty power. Let his death be as precious in Thy eyes, as the uprightness of his life was pleasing to Thee, so that he may depart in peace and in the certain hope of the eternal reward to be given to him on the day in which Thou shalt open the gates

of heaven for all the faithful. Be mindful, my Son, of the humility and love of Thy servant; of his exceeding great merits and virtues; of the fidelity and solicitude by which this just man has supported Thee and me, Thy humble handmaid, in the sweat of his brow."

Our Savior answered: "My Mother, Thy request is pleasing to Me, and the merits of Joseph are acceptable in My eyes. I will now assist him and will assign him a place among the princes of My people, so high that he will be the admiration of the angels and will cause them and all men to break forth in highest praise. With none of the human born shall I do as with thy spouse." The great Lady gave thanks to Her sweetest Son for this promise; and, for nine days and nights before the death of Saint Joseph he uninterruptedly enjoyed the company and attendance of Mary or Her divine Son. By command of the Lord the holy angels, three times on each of the nine days, furnished celestial music, mixing their hymns of praise with the benedictions of the sick man. More over, their humble but most precious dwelling was filled with sweetest fragrance and odors so wonderful that they comforted not only Saint Joseph, but invigorated all the numerous persons who happened to come near the house.

One day before he died, being wholly inflamed with divine love on account of these blessings, he was wrapt in an ecstasy which lasted twenty-four hours. The Lord Himself supplied strength for this miraculous intercourse. In this ecstasy he saw clearly the divine Essence, and, manifested therein, all that he had believed by faith: The incomprehensible Divinity, the mystery of the Incarnation and Redemption, the militant Church with all its Sacraments and mysteries. The Blessed Trinity commissioned and as signed him as the messenger of our Savior to the holy Patriarchs and Prophets of limbo; and commanded him to prepare them for their issuing forth from this bosom of Abraham to eternal rest and happiness. All this, most holy Mary saw reflected in the soul

of Her divine Son together with all the other mysteries, just as they had been made known to Her beloved spouse, and She offered Her sincerest thanks for all this to Her Lord.

When Saint Joseph issued from this ecstasy his face shone with wonderful splendor and his soul was entirely transformed by his vision of the essence of God. He asked his blessed Spouse to give him Her benediction; but She requested Her divine Son to bless him in Her stead, which He did. Then the great Queen of humility, falling on Her knees, besought Saint Joseph to bless Her, as being Her husband and head. Not without divine impulse the man of God fulfilled this request for the consolation of his most prudent Spouse. She kissed the hand with which he blessed Her and asked him to salute the just ones of limbo in Her name. The most humble Joseph, sealing his life with an act of self-abasement, asked pardon of his heavenly Spouse for all his deficiencies in Her service and love and begged Her to grant him Her assistance and intercession in this hour of his passing away. The holy man also rendered humblest thanks to Her Son for all the blessings of his life and especially for those received during this sickness. The last words which Saint Joseph spoke to his Spouse were: "Blessed art Thou among all women and elect of all the creatures. Let angels and men praise thee; let all the generations know, praise and exalt thy dignity; and may in thee be known, adored and exalted the name of the Most High through all the coming ages; may He be eternally praised for having created thee so pleasing in His eyes and in the sight of all the blessed spirits. I hope to enjoy thy sight in the heavenly fatherland."

Then this man of God, turning toward Christ, our Lord, in profoundest reverence, wished to kneel before Him. But the sweetest Jesus, coming near, received him in His arms, where, reclining his head upon them Joseph said: "My highest Lord and God, Son of the Eternal Father, Creator and Redeemer of the world, give Thy blessing to Thy servant and the work of Thy hand; pardon, O most merciful King, the faults which I have committed in Thy service and intercourse. I extol and magnify Thee and render eternal and heartfelt thanks to Thee for having, in Thy ineffable condescension, chosen me to be the spouse of Thy true Mother; let Thy greatness and glory be my thanksgiving for all eternity." The Redeemer of the world gave him His benediction, saying: "My father, rest in peace and in the grace of My Eternal Father and thine; and to the Prophets and Saints, who await thee in limbo, bring the joyful news of the approach of their redemption." At these words of Jesus, and reclining in His arms, the most fortunate Saint Joseph expired, and the Lord Himself closed his eyes. At the same time the multitude of the angels, who attended upon their King and Queen, intoned hymns of praise in loud and harmonious voices. By command of the Lord they carried his most holy soul to the gathering-place of the Patriarchs and Prophets, where it was immediately recognized by all as clothed in the splendors of incomparable grace, as the putative father and the intimate friend of the Redeemer, worthy of highest veneration. Conformably to the will and mandate of the Lord, his arrival spread unutterable joy in this countless gathering of the saints by the announcement of their speedy rescue.

It is necessary to mention that the long sickness and sufferings which preceded the death of Saint Joseph were not the sole cause and occasion of his passing away; for with all his infirmities he could have extended the term of his life, if to them he had not joined the fire of the intense love within his bosom. In order that his death might be more the triumph of his love than of the effects of original sin, the Lord suspended the special and miraculous assistance by which his natural forces were enabled to withstand the violence of his love during his lifetime. As soon as this divine assistance was withdrawn, nature was overcome by his love and the bonds and chains, by which this most holy soul was detained in its mortal body, were at once dissolved and the separation of the soul from the body in which death consists took place. Love was then the real cause of the death of Saint Joseph, as I have said above. This was at the same time the greatest and most glorious of all his infirmities for in it death is but a sleep of the body and the beginning of real life.

Our Lady instructs us on the hour of death: "At the point of death the souls of men incur the most incredible and dangerous attacks from the demons, as well as from their own frailty and from the creatures around them. That hour is the great trial of life, upon which depends the last sentence of eternal death or eternal life. I exhort thee to exert all thy powers and faculties to act accordingly. Remember, then, my friend, that when Lucifer and his satellites of darkness perceive, by the course of natural events, that any one falls a prey to a dangerous and mortal disease, they immediately prepare to assail the poor and unbewaring soul with all their malice and astuteness in order to vanquish them

if possible by various temptations. Whenever they see an opening for attacking the souls, they try to supply in fury and malice the shortness of time.

"At such times they gather like blood-thirsty wolves and search out the natural and acquired failings in his nature, taking into account his inclinations, habits and customs, and where his passions cause him greater weakness, in order to direct toward this part the strongest battery and engines of war. Those that have a disorderly love of earthly life, they persuade that there is not such great danger and they prevent others from undeceiving them. Those that have been negligent in the reception of the Sacraments, they try to make still more careless and they place obstacles and difficulties in the way in order that they may receive them without fruit and with a bad disposition. Others they fill with false suggestions and shame in order that they may not confess their sins and open their conscience. Others, who love vanity, they entangle, even at that last hour, in many vain and proud desires with regard to what is to be done for them after death. Those that have been avaricious or sensual, they seek to excite violently toward what they loved so blindly during life. In short, of all the bad habits and customs this cruel enemy avails himself in order to fill their minds with images of creatures and draw them away from their salvation or make them incapable of it. All the sinful actions and vicious habits of their previous life have become, as it were, pledges in the hands of the common enemy for the possession of the sinner and weapons for assault and battery in this tremendous hour of death. Every appetite, which has been inordinately indulged, is an avenue or bypath by which he enters into the citadel of the soul. Once in, he breathes forth his pestilential fumes, and raises the clouds of darkness, his proper work, so that the soul may not give heed to the divine inspirations, have no true sorrow for its sins, and do no penance for its wicked life.

"**G**enerally these enemies cause a great damage to the souls in that hour by exciting the vain hope of a longer life and being able to execute later on what God suggests to them by means of the holy angels. Giving way to this deceit, they find themselves afterwards betrayed and lost. Just as great is the danger of those who have shown little esteem for the saving graces of the Sacraments: for this contempt is very offensive to the Lord and to the saints, and divine justice is wont to punish it by leaving these souls to their own wicked counsels. This leads them to great neglect in profiting by this help. Thus they are themselves forsaken by the Lord in their last hour, in which they expected to provide for their salvation. There are few among the just whom this ancient serpent does not furiously attack in their last agony. And if satan boasts of having ruined even saints at such times, what hope have the wicked, the negligent and sinful, who have spent their whole lives in making themselves unworthy of divine favor and grace and who are devoid of meritorious works, to offset the assaults of their enemies? My holy spouse, Saint Joseph, was one of those who enjoyed the privilege of neither seeing nor feeling the presence of the demon in his last hour; for as soon as they approached to deal with him as they do with the rest of men, they felt a powerful force, which kept them at a distance and the holy angels hurled them back into their abyss. Seeing themselves thus oppressed and crushed, they were seized with great uneasiness and confusion.

"**H**ence thou wilt understand the great danger in the hour of death, when both the good works and the bad will begin to show their effects. I will not tell thee how many

are thus lost, in order that thy sincere love of God may not cause thee to die of sorrow at this loss. But the general rule is: a good life gives hope of a good end; all other reliance is doubtful, and salvation resting upon it is very rare and merely accidental. The best precaution is to take a good start from afar; and therefore I admonish thee, that, at the dawning of each day, when thou lookest upon the light, thou seriously consider whether it may not be the last of thy life, and, if it should be the last (for thou dost not know), that thou place thy soul in such a state as to be able to meet death with a smiling face. Do not delay even for one instant sorrow for thy sins and a firm purpose of confessing them as soon as thou findest thyself guilty of any and of amending the least of thy imperfections. In all this be so careful that thou leave not upon thy conscience the smallest defect without being sorry for it and without cleansing thyself by the blood of my most holy Son. Place thyself in such a condition that thou art ready to appear before the just Judge, Who is to examine and judge thy least thoughts and all thy movements."

Why God Selected Him

The most fortunate of men, Saint Joseph, reached an age of sixty years and a few days. For at the age of thirty-three he espoused the Blessed Virgin and he lived with Her a little longer than twenty-seven years as Her husband. When Saint Joseph died, She had completed the half of Her forty-second year; for She was espoused to Saint Joseph at the age of fourteen.

The heavenly Lady was either the instrumental or meritorious cause of the holiness of Her spouse, or at least the final object or purpose of this holiness. For all the vast perfection of his virtues and graces were conferred upon Saint Joseph for the purpose of making of him a worthy protector and spouse of Her, whom God selected as His Mother. According to this standard and according to the love of God for His most holy Mother is to be measured the holiness of Saint Joseph; if there had been in the world another man more perfect and more worthy, the Lord would have chosen this other one for the spouse of His Mother. Since he was chosen by God, Saint Joseph was no doubt the most perfect man upon earth. Having created and destined him for such a high end, it is certain that God, in His almighty power, prepared and perfected him in proportion to the exaltedness of his end. That is (according to our way of thinking), his holiness, virtues, gifts, graces and infused and natural habits were made to correspond by divine influence with the end for which he was selected.

There was a certain difference in the graces given to this great Patriarch and those vouchsafed to other saints; for many saints were endowed with graces and gifts that are intended not for the increase of their own sanctity, but for the advance of the service of the Most High in other souls; freely given and not dependent upon the godliness of the receiver. But in our blessed Patriarch all the divine favors were productive of personal virtue and perfection; for the mysterious purpose, toward which they tended and helped along, was closely connected with the holiness of his own life. The more angelic and holy he grew to be, so much the more worthy was he to be the spouse of most holy Mary, the depository and treasure-house of heavenly sacraments. He was to be a miracle of holiness, as he really was. His marvelous holiness commenced with the formation of his body in the womb of his mother. In this the providence of God Himself interfered, regulating the composition of the four radical humors of his body with extreme nicety of proportion and securing for him that evenly tempered disposition which made his body a blessed earth fit for the abode of an exquisite soul and well-balanced mind. He was sanctified in the womb of his mother seven months after his conception, and the leaven of sin was destroyed in him for the whole course of his life, never having felt any impure or disorderly movement. Although he did not receive the use of his reason together with this first sanctification, which consisted principally in justification from original sin, yet his mother at the time felt a wonderful joy of the Holy Ghost. Without understanding entirely the mystery, she elicited great acts of virtue and believed that her son, or whomever she bore in her womb, would be wonderful in the sight of God and men.

The holy child Joseph was born most beautiful and perfect of body and caused in his parents and in his relations an extraordinary delight, something like that caused by the birth of Saint John the Baptist, though the cause of it was more hidden. The Lord hastened in him the use of his reason, perfecting it in his third year, endowing it with infused science and augmenting his soul with new graces and virtues. From that time the child began to know God by faith, and also by natural reasoning and science; as the cause and Author of all things. He eagerly listened and understood profoundly all that was taught him in regard to God and His works. At this immature age he already practiced the highest kinds of prayer and contemplation and eagerly engaged in the exercise of the virtues proper to his youth; so that, at the time when others come to the use of reason, at the age of seven years or more, Saint Joseph was already a perfect man in the use of it and in holiness. He was of a kind disposition, loving, affable, sincere, showing inclinations not only holy but angelic, growing in virtue and perfection and advancing toward his espousal with most holy Mary by an altogether irreproachable life.

For the confirmation and increase of his good qualities was then added the intercession of the blessed Lady; for as soon as She was informed that the Lord wished Her to enter the married state with him, She earnestly besought

the Lord to sanctify Saint Joseph and inspire him with most chaste thoughts and desires in conformity with Her own. The Lord listened to Her prayer and permitted Her to see what great effects His right hand wrought in the mind and spirit of the patriarch Saint Joseph. They were so copious, that they cannot be described in human words. He infused into his soul the most perfect habits of all the virtues and gifts. He balanced anew all his faculties and filled him with grace, confirming it in an admirable manner. In the virtue and perfection of chastity the holy spouse was elevated higher than the seraphim; for the purity, which they possessed without body, Saint Joseph possessed in his earthly body and in mortal flesh; never did an image of the impurities of the animal and sensible nature engage, even for one moment, any of his faculties. This freedom from all such imaginations and his angelic simplicity fitted him for the companionship and presence of the most Pure among all creatures, and without this excellence he would not have been worthy of so great a dignity and rare excellence.

Also in the other virtues he was wonderfully distinguished, especially in charity; for he dwelt at the fountainhead of that living water, which flows on to eternal life (John 4:14); he was in close proximity to that sphere of fire and was consumed without resistance. The best that can be said of the charity of our saint is what I have already said in the preceding chapter; namely, that his love of God was really the cause of his mortal sickness and of his death.

The manner of his death was a privilege of his singular love, for his sweet sighs of love surpassed and finally put an end to those of his sickness, being far more powerful. As

the objects of his love, Christ and His Mother, were present with him always and as both of Them were more close-ly bound to him than to any of the woman-born, his most pure and faith-ful heart was unavoid-ably consumed by the loving effects of such a close union. Blessed be the Author of such great wonders and blessed be the most fortunate of mortals, Saint Joseph, who so worthily corre-sponded to their love. He deserves to be known and extolled by all the gener-ations of men and all na-tions, since the Lord has wrought such things with no other man and to none has He shown such love.

Saint Joseph had many divine visions and rev elations and the greatest of them all was his having known the mysteries of the relation between Christ and His Mother and his having lived in Their company for so many years as the putative father of the Lord and as the true spouse of the Queen of heaven. There are certain other privileges conferred upon Saint Joseph by the Most High on account of his great holiness, which are especially important to those who ask his intercession in a proper manner. In virtue of these special privileges the intercession of Saint Joseph is most powerful: first, for attaining the virtue of purity and overcoming the sensual inclinations of the flesh; secondly, for procuring powerful help to escape sin and return to the friendship of God; thirdly, for increasing the love and devotion to most holy Mary; fourthly, for securing the grace of a happy death and protection against the demons in that hour; fifthly, for inspiring the demons with terror at the mere mention of his name by his clients; sixthly, for gaining health of body and assistance in all kinds of difficulties; seventhly, for securing issue of children in families. These and many other favors God confers upon those who properly and with good disposition seek the intercession of the spouse of our Queen, Saint Joseph. I beseech all the faithful children of the Church to be very devout to him and they will experience these favors in reality, if they dispose themselves, as they should in order to receive and merit them.

"I do not remember that I ever asked him at any time for anything which he did not obtain for me."

—St. Teresa of Avila

Our Lady appeared to St. Simon Stock in 1251 with the Scapular Garment in her hand and said: "This shall be to you and all Carmelites a privilege, that anyone who dies clothed in this shall not suffer eternal fire; and if wearing it they die, they shall be saved.

THE *Blessed Virgin Mary*
—SPOUSE OF *St. Joseph*

Now also honored as

Our Lady of
MOUNT CARMEL

or

Our Lady of the
BROWN SCAPULAR

These visions* are brief and they succeed one another rapidly. Three times St. Joseph has traced the sign of the cross above the people. St. Joseph fades away, and Christ appears at the base of the sun. He is cloaked in red. With Him stands His Mother. She is gowned now in neither white nor blue, but as Our Lady of Sorrows, gazing on the earth. She has not the traditional sword in her heart. This the children clearly note, and are later able to recall. Christ gives his blessing to the people, and then, as this vision passes, there is one that Lucia alone is privileged to see: Our Lady of Mount Carmel.

---

* Seen during climactic Miracle of the Sun at Fatima, Oct 13, 1917

Saint Joseph is the Patron of the Universal Church. Pope Pius IX reasoned that he must be the special protector of the Family of the Church now, even as he was appointed by God to be the protector of the Family at Nazareth. But what does Mary do with the Scapular but render Herself, and Saint Joseph, particularly our protectors and our patrons, to the extent that we cannot be lost? By the Scapular, which constitutes a true devotion to his most pure spouse, St. Joseph exercises this patronage in a very special way.

Of all the benefits that flow from the Scapular, this benefit of being the special children of Saint Joseph is one of the greatest. After an assurance of Mary's presence in life, at death and after death, what could be more desirable than the continual love and special protection of the greatest Saint in Heaven?

Now, when either husband or wife adopts children, as Mary has adopted us by Her Scapular contract, those children are naturally also those of the spouse. Hence, Saint Joseph is especially the father of the Scapular family. There was never a marital union more purely intense than that which was divinely contracted by Providence between Mary and Joseph. It was a union of two hearts for the greatest work of all time, intensified by a common love for a Divine Infant, Our Salvation. Hence, that children adopted by Mary *in an assurance of salvation* should become the special children of Saint Joseph is even more certain than that adopted children in general should become the children of the foster father as well as of the mother.

But Mary and Joseph have not adopted special children by the Scapular Promise simply that these children may increase the number of their devotees in the Church. Their reasons for the establishment of that vast family—united by a perfect, wordless devotion—are deep and, in their fullness, almost unsoundable. But of one reason we can be certain. They have wrought this work of centuries, from days of prophecy down to the present day, because *they wish to establish the Reign of their Infant God*, the Eucharistic King. That reign is to come about through Mary. Since Jesus dwells here on earth in our tabernacles, He can come to reign in the manner most pleasing to Him if Mary's children imitate Saint Joseph and establish the reign of the Sacred Heart in their hearts, by uniting themselves to Mary.

After Joseph had learned that his spouse bore the Son of the Eternal God, how he must have sought Mary's company and longed to talk with Her about Jesus, about how they would teach the Son of God to walk, embrace Him, how they would care for Him. These must have been moments of great, great joy as well as of love and understanding—for Mary and Joseph.

Today, when the Son of God is being born again, born in the hearts of His redeemed, can we believe that Joseph is not discussing, in Heaven, "the coming of Jesus a second time through Her?" Is it not also Joseph's work, Joseph's task? Most certainly! Joseph stands as the model for the modern man: in poverty, in industry, in temperance, in union with Mary. And not only is he a model, but he actually engenders in us these virtues which are so hard to discover in the rush of modern "civilization." It was at the so-called Reformation, started by Luther, that our present troubles originated in defection from the Church. And when Our Lord then appeared to the great Saint Teresa and said, "My daughter, the ruse of the demon is to remove from the defectors all that would awaken in them the love of God, and, more than ever, My faithful ones must follow the direct opposite way." Saint Teresa says: "I suddenly understood how much *I was obliged to honor the Blessed Virgin and Saint Joseph!*"[4] And when another of the most glorious saints of Our Lady of the Scapular, Mary Magdalen de Pazzi, was given to see the glory of Saint Joseph in an ecstasy, she cried out: "Joseph, united as he is to Jesus and Mary, is like a bright shining star that protects *those souls who fight the battle of life under Mary's standard!*"[5] Oh, that the whole world will soon discover that both Mary and Joseph are hidden in a humble Marian garment worn by millions. That Sign

82

of Salvation, a stumbling block to all the vast armies of Hell, seems to cry out an assurance to the saintly Pius IX who exclaimed—half in wonder, half in awe—"If Joseph and Mary regain the place they should never have lost, the world will again be saved!"[6]

"Back to Nazareth" is, and must be, our cry. Where God Himself—under Mary and Joseph—set an example to the world, we can acquire the force to come forth over the entire world to defend our Christian families with the arms of humility, prayer, chastity and fidelity. God will render us victorious.

THE HOUSE
OF *St. Joseph*

The Holy House of Nazareth is a simple but solid construction of stone, not of brick. It has no foundations, but rests on unprepared ground. Experienced builders declare that it was not built on this site; therefore it was carried from the Holy Land to its present site in Loreto, Italy, 150 miles from Rome. This transportation could only have been miraculous. Together with the House were brought the crucifix of wood and cloth, the plate and the cups in terra cotta, and the altar stone which is under the present altar.

Here the Word was made Flesh.

This was Mary's home, small, dark, with uneven walls, but rich in mysteries and miracles. The preservation of this Holy House is a visible blessing to which fathers and mothers can constantly turn their eyes, meditating upon its silent lessons and modeling their homes to the example given by that most Holy Family which lived therein.

In 1852 Pope Pius IX declared the Holy House of Loreto "is in reality the House of Nazareth... separated from its foundation... where the Most Blessed Virgin was conceived, born, brought up; where Heaven's messenger saluted her as full of grace and blessed among women; where she became the

Mother of the only Son of God.." Pope John XXIII later prayed: "May this Shrine of Loreto be always like a window opened to the world to recall souls to the sanctification of family life." Certainly this Holy House often found place in Pope John's meditations during his daily fifteen mysteries of the Rosary.

ALTAR AND LAMPS NOW GRACE HOLY HOUSE INTERIOR WALLS

The Angels first brought this House from Palestine to Dalmatia, to Tersatto, in the year 1291 when Nicolas IV was Pope. Three years later, during the reign of Boniface VIII, the House was again carried by angels to a wood in Piceno, near the town of Recanati and there within the space of one year it changed position three times. It has stood on its present site for the past three hundred years winning fame as a local marvel and later on becoming renowned throughout the world for the fame of its miracles. Today, after so many centuries the same walls still stand, without foundations yet whole and entire, and the Holy House is venerated by all nations. It was enclosed in splendid marble by Pope Clement VII in the year 1534. Pope Clement VIII in 1595 ordered that a short account of the wonderful Translation of the House should be inscribed on the marble.

HIGHEST *Praise* AND *Honor*

Fifty years after St. Joseph had been proclaimed Patron of the Universal Church by Pope Pius IX, Pope Benedict XV, in 1920, selected him as the patron of workmen.

✴ ✴ ✴

BLESSED VIRGIN MARY TO ST. BRIDGET OF SWEDEN

"St. Joseph was so reserved and careful in his speech, that not one word ever issued from his mouth that was not good and holy, nor did he ever indulge in unnecessary or less charitable conversation. He was most patient and diligent in bearing fatigue; he practiced extreme poverty; he was most meek in bearing injuries; he was strong and constant against my enemies; he was the faithful witness of the wonders of Heaven, being dead to the flesh and the world, living only for God and for heavenly goods, which were the only things he de sired. He was perfectly conformed to the Divine Will and so resigned to the dispositions of Heaven, that he ever repeated: 'May the Will of God ever be done in me!' He rarely spoke with men, but continually with God, Whose Will he desired to per form. Wherefore, he now enjoys great glory in Heaven."

✣ ✣ ✣

St. Teresa of Avila

During an illness in which no earthly physician was able to give her relief, St. Teresa decided to implore the blessed in Heaven to restore her health. She writes: "I chose for my patron and lord the glorious St. Joseph, and I recommended myself earnestly to him. I saw that, both from this my present trouble, and from those of greater consequence relating to my honor and the loss of my soul, this my father and lord delivered me and rendered me greater services than I knew how to ask for. I do not remember that I ever asked him at any time for anything which he did not obtain for me. It fills me with amazement when I consider the numberless graces which God has granted me through the intercession of this blessed saint and the perils, both of body and soul, from which he has delivered me.

"To other saints the Most High seems to have given grace to succor men in some special necessity, but this glorious saint, I know by experience, has power to help us in all. Our Lord wishes us to understand by this that as He Himself was subject to St. Joseph while on earth, recognizing in him the authority of foster father and guardian, so now in Heaven He is pleased to grant all his requests.

✣ ✣ ✣

Now the divine house which Joseph ruled with the authority of a father contained within its limits the scarce-born Church. From the very fact that the most holy Virgin is the Mother of Jesus Christ she is the Mother of all Christians, whom she bore on Mount Calvary amid the supreme throes of the Redemption; Jesus Christ is, in a manner, the Firstborn of Christians, who by adoption and Redemption are His brothers.

And for such reasons the blessed Patriarch looks upon the multitude of Christians who make up the Church as confided especially to his trust — this limitless family spread over the earth, over which, because he is the spouse of Mary and the father of Jesus Christ, he holds, as it were, a paternal authority. It is, then, natural and worthy that as the blessed Joseph ministered to all the needs of the family at Nazareth and girt it about with his protection, he should now cover with the cloak of his heavenly patronage and defend the Church of Jesus Christ.

✷ ✷ ✷

PIUS XI: *Divini Redemptoris*

On March 19, 1937, the Feast of St. Joseph, Pope Pius XI's Encyclical Letter (***Divini Redemptoris***), "On Atheistic Communism," was promulgated. Its concluding paragraphs declared St. Joseph to be the patron of the struggle against atheistic communism:

"To hasten the advent of that 'peace of Christ in the kingdom of Christ' so ardently desired by all, We place the vast campaign of the Church against world Communism under the standard of St. Joseph, her mighty Protector. He belongs to the working-class, and he bore the burdens of poverty for himself and the Holy Family, whose tender and vigilant head he was. To him was entrusted the Divine Child when Herod loosed his assassins against Him. In a life of faithful performance of everyday duties, he left an example for all those who must gain their bread by the toil of their hands. He won for himself the title of 'The Just', serving thus as a living model of that Christian justice which should reign in social life.

"With eyes lifted on high, Our Faith sees the new heavens and the new earth described by Our first Predecessor, St. Peter. While the promises of the false prophets of this earth melt away in blood and tears, the great apocalyptic prophecy of the Redeemer shines forth in heavenly splendor: 'Behold, I make all things new.'"

✳ ✳ ✳

O glorious Patriarch, St. Joseph, humble and just crafts man of Nazareth, who gave to all Christians, but particularly to us, an example of a perfect life of assiduous work and of admirable unity with Mary and Jesus, help us in our daily work so that we also, Catholic workmen, may find therein an effective means of glorifying our Lord, of sanctifying ourselves, and of being useful to the society in which we live—the supreme ideal of all our actions.

Obtain for us from our Lord, O beloved protector, humility and simplicity of heart, attachment to work, benevolence toward those who work with us, compliance with the Divine Will in the difficulties of this life and joy in bearing them, consciousness of our specific social mission and sense of our social responsibility, a spirit of discipline and prayer, docility and respect for our superiors, fraternity toward our equals, charity and indulgence for our dependents.

Be with us in prosperous times when everything invites us to enjoy the fruits of our labor in a seemly manner, but be our support also in times of stress when the skies seem to close in upon us and even the tools of our work seem to rebel in our hands.

Grant that, following your example, we may hold fast to Mary, our Mother, your gentle spouse who was content to work quietly in a corner of your humble shop, that we may never turn our eyes from Jesus, who toiled with you at your carpenter's bench, so that we may lead a peaceful and holy life on earth, the prelude to that eternally happy one which awaits us in heaven forevermore. Amen.

SAN JOSÉ NUESTRO PROTECTOR.
Oh santo Protector mio, ha llegado la hora.
abridme la puerta del cielo.

Jesus, Mary and Joseph,

I give you my heart and my soul.

Jesus, Mary and Joseph, assist me in

my last agony.

Jesus, Mary and Joseph, let me breathe

forth my spirit in peace with you.

—The Raccolta

St. Joseph AND FATIMA [7]

$\mathcal{A}$t Fatima on October 13, 1917, St. Joseph appeared holding the Child Jesus in his arms, and he and Jesus blessed the people. Not a word was spoken, yet the message was clear: little Jesus has complete trust in St. Joseph and so was honored to be lifted up before the eyes of the world by him. Our priests lift up to us the consecrated Body and Blood of Jesus at the Mass. Many great saints have spent many long hours with Jesus in Eucharist Adoration, but St. Joseph spent the time from Jesus' birth to the time of his own death in perpetual adoration of Jesus in the company of Mary.

In a 16th century prophecy, Isidore of Isolanis, a pious Dominican, said that the sound of victory will be heard in the Church Militant when the faithful recognize the sanctity of St. Joseph. He continues: "The Lord will let His light shine, He will lift the veil, and great men will search out the interior gifts of God that are hidden in St. Joseph; they will find in him a priceless treasure, the like of which they had never found in other saints of the Old Testament. We are inclined to believe that toward the end of time God will overwhelm St. Joseph with glorious honors. If in the past ages, during the storms of persecution, these honors could not be shown to St. Joseph, we must conclude that they have been reserved for later times.

At some future time the feast of St. Joseph will be celebrated as one of the greatest feasts. The Vicar of Christ, inspired by the Holy Spirit, will order this feast to be celebrated in the Universal Church."

For the most part, St. Joseph is unknown even among Catholics. Why? Because he is hidden even more than Mary, and Mary is a "garden enclosed," as is St. Joseph, being her most holy and most chaste spouse. But with Fatima, and discerning the "signs of the times," there is indication that now is the time for the glories of St. Joseph to become known.

Who is St. Joseph? He is the worthy, most chaste spouse of the Blessed Virgin Mary. It was God Himself - the Most Holy Trinity - Who destined St. Joseph to be the spouse of the Blessed Virgin

Mary, and it was the Holy Trinity Who gave St. Joseph all the qualities necessary to be the foster father of Jesus.

St. Joseph was the lawful father of Jesus, and our Blessed Mother did not hesitate to give him that title. We recall in the Fifth Joyful Mystery of the holy Rosary when Jesus was lost, Mary and Joseph found Him in the temple. Mary said to Jesus, "Behold, thy father and I have sought thee sorrowing." Mary did not say, "Behold, thy stepfather and I sought thee sorrowing." Mary honored St. Joseph with the title of father. St. Joseph represented God the Father, and God the Father willed that St. Joseph be called father to His Only-Begotten Son. In Ephesians 3:14f, St. Paul affirms, "For this reason I kneel before the Father, from whom all fatherhood in Heaven and on earth is named."

The Holy Spirit gave to St. Joseph his spouse, the Blessed Virgin Mary. Our Lady, in giving St. Joseph her hand in marriage, also gave him her heart. Never did a wife love her husband more tenderly and lovingly and honor him more profoundly than did Our Lady for St. Joseph.

According to the Church Fathers, he that preserves intact the treasury of virginity ranks as high as the angels. To what degree of holiness must have St. Joseph attained who was the first to preserve virginity in the state of marriage and with such fidelity.

God the Father also gave St. Joseph a father's heart with the love and the authority of a father. St. Joseph, a man created by God, was given authority over Jesus, the second Person of the Blessed Trinity. What a mystery! St. Joseph was the earthly superior of Jesus and Mary as he was husband and father; Jesus and Mary's submission to St. Joseph was so great and complete as to enrapture the angels! St. Joseph, on whom Mary depended and from whom she took direction, had authority over her. What must the angels have thought when they saw St. Joseph command the little King Jesus, and when they beheld Jesus sleeping in his arms?!

We must ask St. Joseph to be our intercessor seeing that he has a singular influence with the two authorities of Heaven and earth, Jesus and Mary. Since he is the lawful father and guardian of Jesus, the chaste spouse and guardian of Mary, what can be refused to the man who produces titles so valid and authentic as these?! Besides, whatever Jesus demands from His Heavenly Father, the Father wills. Whatever our Lady demands from her beloved Son, the Son wills. And whatever St. Joseph demands from his holy spouse, she wills. Does it not follow then that as Mary is all-powerful through Jesus, Joseph is all-powerful through Mary. O, how good it is to have St. Joseph as our advocate, since nothing is impossible for him.

Fortunate is the soul who has devotion to St. Joseph, for devotion to St. Joseph is one of the choicest graces that God can give to a soul. When God wants to raise a soul to greater heights, he unites that soul to St. Joseph by giving that soul a strong love for the good saint. May we increase our love and trust in Jesus, Mary, and St. Joseph.

For the material in this article, and to find out more about the wonders of St. Joseph and his relevance for our times, you may refer to the following sources:

- *Life of St. Joseph* by Sr. Maria Baij.

- *31 Day Novena to St. Joseph* edited by Dr. Rosalie Turton at 101foundation.com.

- *The Man God Called Father* by Promise of Peace 1917 Publishing.

- *Divine Favors Granted to Saint Joseph* by Father Etienne Binet, SJ.

PRAYERS TO Saint Joseph

O, St. Joseph, whose protection is so great, so strong, so prompt before the throne of God, I place in you all my interest and desires.

O, St. Joseph, do assist me by your powerful intercession, and obtain for me from your divine Son all spiritual blessings, through Jesus Christ, Our Lord. So that, having engaged here below your Heavenly power, I may offer my thanksgiving and homage to the most loving of Fathers.

O, St. Joseph, I never weary contemplating you, and Jesus asleep in your arms; I dare not approach while He reposes near your heart. Press Him in my name and kiss His fine head for me and ask Him to return the kiss when I draw my dying breath. St. Joseph, patron of departing souls – pray for me.

*S*t. Joseph, pray for us.

THE MORNING OFFERING

O my God, in union with the Immaculate Heart of Mary (kiss your scapular as a sign of your consecration), I offer Thee the Most Precious Blood of Jesus, present in all the tabernacles of the world, joining with it the offering of my every thought, word and action of this day.

O my Jesus, I desire today to gain every indulgence and merit I can and I offer them, together with myself, to Mary Immaculate, that she may best apply them to the interest of Thy most Sacred Heart. Precious Blood of Jesus, save us! Immaculate Heart of Mary, pray for us! Sacred Heart of Jesus, have mercy on us!

CONSECRATION

O Mary my Queen, my Mother, I give myself entirely to thee, and to show my devotion to thee, I consecrate to thee this day, my eyes, my ears, my mouth, my heart, my whole being without reserve. Therefore, good Mother, as I am thine own, keep me, guard me as thy property and possession. Amen.

Endnotes

1. Born in 1602, Sister Mary of Agreda bilocated to what is now the American southwest and Mexico. She visited the Jumano Indians, encouraging them to go and invite Franciscan missionary priests to come and bring them the Catholic Faith. https://www.nps.gov/sapu/learn/historyculture/maria-de-agreda.htm

—*The Publisher*, 2024

2. An English land-league contains approximately three statute miles. A statute mile is the regular mile of 5,280 ft. Therefore 200 leagues is 3 x 200 or about 600 miles.

3. 30 leagues is 3 x 30 or about 90 miles.

4. *Letters*, Ed. P. Gregoire, III, rel. ix, pg. 402.

5. Huguet, *The Power of St. Joseph*: pg. 130.

6. Ibidem, Med. 30.

7. Additional material on St. Joseph by *The Publisher*, 2024.

FIRST SATURDAYS
OF REPARATION

"First Saturdays of Reparation"

As requested by Our Lady of Fatima

Monthly Prayer Devotion

Dear Friends of Jesus, Mary and Joseph, ————————

This beautiful little book has been designed so that every parish can pray together each "First Saturday" of every month the Most Holy Rosary and the Prayers Our Blessed Mother asked for. These First Saturday prayers and devotions are to be offered in reparation for the blasphemies against the Immaculate Heart of Mary. Her urgent requests also include monthly Holy Communion and Confession within seven days of that First Saturday.

This little book will help us **pray together as a group**, or as **individuals**, the prayers and petitions to Our Lord and Our Lady that she requested at her Fatima Apparitions.

Therefore, let us all put forth a great effort to invite our friends, families and associates to start a **"First Saturday of Reparation" in all of our parishes**.

Thank you.

———— In Jesus through Mary ————

Helen Miller
promiseofpeace1917@gmail.com
Diocese of Marquette, Michigan
Mother of Perpetual Help Mission Parish
Member of World Apostolate of Fatima / Blue Army

9 79988 691 3 2048